grow
the handbook for christian growth

The Handbook for Christian Growth

Design: David Riley Associates
Typesetting: David Riley Associates
Copywriting: Leah Case
Copyediting: Harvest Publications

Printed in the United States of America.

ISBN-13: 978-1-932778-32-8

Visit Harvest Ministries' award winning Web site at harvest.org.

TABLE OF CONTENTS

A WORD FROM PASTOR GREG

Dear Friend,

Are you serving the Lord?

I believe that God has called every Christian into service. Not everyone is called to be a pastor, an evangelist, or a missionary, but I do believe that we are called to serve the Lord with the gifts God has given us. That is where the greatest fulfillment in life comes from.

God's desire for His children to serve Him is illustrated in the account of the Exodus. God went through drastic measures to free His people from Egyptian bondage. He didn't do it so they could go off and do whatever they wanted. Instead, God freed His people so they could serve Him (see Exodus 7:16).

At the same time, it's important to be fully prepared so you can serve God most effectively. You wouldn't make a five-course meal without knowing how to cook or which kitchen equipment to use. And you wouldn't take apart the engine of your car unless you knew how to put it back together again.

That's where *The Handbook for Christian Growth* comes in. This book is designed to help you discover your spiritual gifts and learn the essentials of Scripture so that you can minister to people to the best of your God-given gifts and abilities. Once you've completed the lessons, I believe you'll understand your faith better and be ready to put your talents to work in the service of God.

I pray that this resource will give you a firm foundation in your faith in Christ. May it also equip you to serve God and His church in the world.

Greg Laurie

grow

INTRODUCTION

"As you therefore have received Christ Jesus the Lord, so walk in Him, rooted and built up in Him and established in the faith, as you have been taught, abounding in it with thanksgiving." (Colossians 2:6–7)

In Christian life, growth is a constant process of taking in and giving out. It is a great day when we see the vital connection between learning and serving, when we discover that God has called us to fill a place—not just take up space! The fact that you are reading this handbook indicates you have a desire to grow in your faith and serve the Lord. That's a desire He promises to fulfill. As you dig into God's Word and practice what you learn, you will be like a tree firmly planted by rivers of water, bearing fruit in season (see Psalm 1:3).

A tree's growth and fruitfulness depends on a strong root system. Roots anchor the tree so that it will stand strong through any storm. They draw moisture and nutrients from the soil so the tree can thrive and produce. Though unseen, the root spread of a tree generally needs to be equal to the spread of its branches. By comparison, our ability to minister to others is greatly increased when the roots of our understanding are deep and widespread.

This handbook is designed to help you grow in your knowledge of God's Word so that—like a well-rooted, fruit-bearing tree—you will be established in faith and fruitful in service.

This book can be used for group or individual study. Each chapter is divided into three parts:

1. **Rooted and Built Up.** Read the information and complete the interactive exercise.

2. **Established in the Faith.** Follow the outline, reading each verse and prayerfully considering each point. You may want to use the notes section as a personal journal.

3. **Abounding.** Reflect and respond to each question.

At the end of each chapter, you will find a list of recommended resources, as well as useful charts and information on the chapter topic.

grow

HOW TO STUDY THE BIBLE CHAPTER 1

ROOTED AND BUILT UP

Why study the Bible? The writer of Psalm 119 said, "Oh, how I love your law! I think about it all day long" (Psalm 119:97 NLT).

What did the psalmist see in the pages of God's Word to provoke such a stirring declaration? Simply put, he found food for his soul. Like David, he found God's Word to be sweeter than honey (see Psalm 19:10). Like Job, he treasured God's Word more than his necessary food (see Job 23:12).

Do you like to eat? How is your *spiritual* appetite? Growing Christians need daily nourishment. If we want to know God, and learn to be godly, there is no substitute for consistently feeding on God's Word.

While there are a variety of ways to study the Bible, we can put them into three general categories: directed, discovery, and devotional. For a healthy and balanced spiritual diet, try to incorporate regular "servings" from each category into your study of God's Word.

This chapter is designed to help you become familiar with these methods of Bible study.

Directed Study

Directed study (or deductive Bible study) guides an individual or group into understanding God's Word and relates it to the needs and concerns of life. In a directed Bible study, information is provided by a teacher and/or a written lesson that opens the Scriptures, lays out specific biblical principles, offers food for thought, and encourages spiritual growth through applying God's Word to daily life.

Whenever the Word of God is taught in a sermon, this is also a form of directed Bible study.

Discovery Learning

Discovery learning (or inductive Bible study) encourages believers to explore the great treasure of God's Word for themselves. The writer of Psalm 119 expressed the joy of discovery when he said, "I rejoice at Your word as one who finds great treasure" (Psalm 119:162).

God's Word is an inexhaustible supply of truth and wisdom for living. Have you learned to excavate those riches for yourself? That is the aim of inductive Bible study.

In inductive Bible study, three basic skills are developed and always used:

1. Start with **observation**. *What does it say?* Get involved in what you're reading by asking who, what, when, where types of questions. The point is to gather information, but it need not be a dry, academic process. Let your natural curiosity and desire to learn set the pace. Imagine the people, places, and events you read about. Don't use your imagination to produce facts—use it to bring the biblical facts to life.

2. **Interpretation** looks for meaning without misunderstanding. *What does it mean?* First, we must understand what the writer wanted his original readers to hear. Then we ask how it relates to life today. Some helpful questions to ask: What does this teach about God? What does it say about man? Is there a command to obey? A promise to claim? Is there a warning to heed? Is there an example to follow or avoid? The Bible is filled with principles—the building blocks that form the foundation of what we believe and how we behave toward God and others. Simply put, a principle is a spiritual lesson.

3. **Application** isn't just the last step of inductive study—it's the next step toward spiritual growth. *How does this apply to me?* Application calls for a response. How will you cooperate with God in living what you have learned? The only way to move truth off the pages of your Bible and into your life is to take steps to put it into action.

> *The mark of spiritual maturity is not how much [of the Bible] you understand, but how much you use. In the spiritual realm, the opposite of ignorance is not knowledge but obedience.*
>
> —Howard G. Hendricks and William D. Hendricks, Living By the Book[1]

 grow

GIVE IT A TRY...

Let's look at 2 Timothy 3:16–17 for a brief and simple demonstration of how to use the inductive method. Some of the questions have been answered for you (in parentheses) and space is provided for the questions you will answer. The only tools you need for this beginning exercise are a Bible and a standard dictionary.

> *All Scripture is **inspired** by God and **profitable** for **teaching**, for **reproof**, for **correction**, for **training** in **righteousness**; so that the man of God may be **adequate**, **equipped** for every **good work**. (2 Timothy 3:16–17 NASB)*

Observation: Who is writing? (Paul the Apostle) Who is he writing to? (Timothy, a "true son in the faith," according to 1 Timothy 1:2)

Now it's your turn. Write the definition for each word:

inspired: _____

profitable: _____

teaching: _____

reproof: _____

correction: _____

training: _____

righteousness: _____

adequate: _____

equipped: _____

good work: _____

Who inspired Scripture? What does it do? _____

_____

Interpretation: What does this passage mean? What did Paul want Timothy, and all believers, to understand? Consider:

What does this verse teach about God and His Word? _____

_____

Why should we study the Bible? _____

_____

Two examples of interpretation (a spiritual lesson) would be:

1. The whole Bible is inspired by God.
2. Studying the Bible is profitable in at least four different ways: teaching, reproof, correction, and training.

Application: *How does this apply to me?* When you write an application, it's helpful to put it in the form of a question to ask yourself. Avoid questions that can simply be answered yes or no. An application question should practical. For example: *How will Bible study help me grow in my Christian life?*

Or you may choose to write your application as a statement of how you will put the spiritual lesson into practice. For example: *I will be a consistent and faithful student of God's Word so I will grow.*

Studying the Bible this way is a system anyone can use, no matter what level of spiritual maturity or education you have. With time and practice, you will develop more skills, but the basic three-step process remains the same. The secret to successful discovery learning is not having a head for facts, but having a heart to listen, learn, and obey.

Some practical suggestions:

- Take advantage of the recommended resources listed at the end of this chapter to learn more about inductive study.

- Consider joining an inductive Bible study group where you can learn with others.

Now let's consider a third way to study your Bible.

Devotional Reading

Devotional reading (commonly called "quiet time") focuses on intimate fellowship with God through contemplation of His Word, worship, and prayer. The focus may be on a single verse or a small portion of Scripture. Devotional books can be helpful

for the structure and inspiration they provide, but the goal of devotional reading should always be meditation on God's Word.

In Proverbs 8:34, we get a glimpse of what pleases God: "Blessed is the man who listens to me, watching daily at my gates, waiting at the posts of my doors."

This description of an individual who is listening, watching, and waiting perfectly illustrates what lies at the heart of devotional reading. It is taking time to allow God to speak to you personally. Here are some essentials:

1. **Listen to God's Word.** The word translated as *listen* means, "to give undivided listening attention; to hear spiritually." This emphasizes the need to set aside a time to read and pray without distractions. Ask God for insight as you meditate on what you read. It may be a new discovery or a simple reminder of familiar truths.

2. **Make devotional reading a daily practice.** *Watching daily* conveys the thought of being alert and spiritually ready. Of all the necessary activities that fill our day, none is more vital than time spent with God in His Word. It prepares us to meet the rest of the day.

3. **Heed what you read.** Simply put, the word translated as *waiting* means, "paying careful attention in order to obey." Write down what God has shown you and how you can apply it. You can be certain God will give you the opportunity to use what you have learned!

Some practical suggestions:

- Choose a single Bible verse, or a small portion of Scripture, to read and meditate on. Read enough to get a clear understanding of what the passage means.

- Keep a journal nearby to record what you have read and what the Lord is speaking to you through it. Write out how it applies to you and how you will respond.

- Seal what you have read with prayer, speaking to the Lord about what He has said in His Word.

As with any worthwhile pursuit, studying the Bible requires commitment and a practical strategy. Here are some helpful habits to cultivate:

- **Find a quiet time and place.** Set aside a reasonable amount of time when you can read and pray without distractions.

- **Have a plan.** Do you want to read through the Bible in a year? Study a book of the Bible in-depth? Study a Bible character or a particular topic? Choose from a wealth of available resources or develop your own plan.

- **Keep a record.** Whether you are using a study guide or keeping a journal on your own, record your observations and discoveries.

- **Put what you learn into practice.** Look for ways (immediate and long-term) to apply what you have learned.

"Success or failure in the Christian life is determined by how much of the Bible you get into your heart and mind on a daily basis and how obedient you are to it. Think about that for a moment.

What amazes me are Christians who have known the Lord for many years, yet do not read the Bible. They attend church and Bible studies and listen a little here and there, but they don't actually open the Word of God and read it.

If you want to grow spiritually, then this must become a regular part of your life. It is essential. It is not something you will outgrow, any more than you will outgrow eating or breathing."

—Greg Laurie, For Every Season.[2]

 grow

ESTABLISHED IN THE FAITH

The Benefits and Blessings of Bible Study

Power of God's Word

1. The Bible reveals what is in our heart (see Hebrews 4:12).
2. The Bible equips us for every good work (see 2 Timothy 3:16–17).

Purpose of Studying God's Word

1. To know God and what He requires (see Psalm 25:4–5).
2. To live a holy life (see Psalm 119:11).
3. To gain wisdom and understanding (see Psalm 119:130).
4. To encourage fellow Christians (see Colossians 3:16).
5. To combat false teaching (see 2 Timothy 2:15).
6. To have an answer for the world (see 1 Peter 3:15).

Promises for Those Who Study and Obey God's Word

1. If we know and obey God's Word we will succeed (see Joshua 1:8).
2. We will be useful and productive in life (see Psalm 1:2–3).
3. Our prayers will be answered (see John 15:7).
4. We will be spiritually "happy"—blessed (see Revelation 1:3).

Notes

_____

_____

_____

_____

_____

_____

_____

_____

_____

_____

_____

_____

_____

_____

_____

_____

_____

_____

_____

_____

_____

_____

_____

_____

_____

 ## ABOUNDING

1. According to 2 Timothy 3:16–17, what should every believer expect as a result of studying God's Word? Describe what that requires, in practical terms.

2. What is one thing you can do to improve your personal Bible study skills?

3. What do you find most challenging about studying the Bible? What do you find most rewarding?

grow

Tools for Bible Study

1. **Study Bibles.** These Bibles include study tools such as book introductions, notes, maps, timelines, a partial concordance, and cross-references. Some study Bibles offer more extensive resources, such as historical/cultural background, word studies, topical indexes, and more.

   Note: Be sure the main Bible you use for study is a *translation* rather than a *paraphrase*. A translation comes from the original language, while a paraphrased Bible has been re-worded from a translation. Some translations are word-for-word, meaning the translators sought to use the most accurate English word to translate the original word and sentence structure. Some translations are thought-for-thought, meaning the goal is to convey the original thought as accurately as possible, using modern language. Every translation is, in a sense, an interpretation of the original text. This is why it's important to use several good translations along with Greek and Hebrew study helps. Some good translations include: the New American Standard Bible (NASB), the New International Bible (NIV), the New Living Translation (NLT), the New King James Version (NKJV) and the King James Version (KJV).

2. **Concordance.** A concordance is an exhaustive index, in alphabetical order, of every word in the Bible. It gives each reference where a certain word is used. This is useful for locating particular scriptures or doing a general word study. A concordance with a Greek/Hebrew Dictionary also gives a brief definition of each word in the Bible by referencing the original Hebrew and Greek.

3. **Word Study Books.** Most people are not literate in the Bible's original languages; so scholars have compiled practical references to help the average student understand what a specific biblical word means. Some word studies are laid out in the same format as the Bible, so you can have the original word and definition readily available as you read. Some are laid out in alphabetical order to be used like a dictionary.

4. **Bible Dictionaries and Encyclopedias.** These are formatted in alphabetical order and give detail on words, customs, people, and traditions in the Bible. They offer historical, geographical, cultural, biographical, and archaeological information.

5. **Atlases.** These include Bible maps, pictures, and diagrams that give a better understanding of the biblical world. An atlas is useful for tracking the events and lives of Bible characters and the changing face of Bible lands through the centuries.

6. **Commentaries.** A commentary is a scholarly interpretation of the Bible. Its purpose is to explain, interpret, and sometimes apply the meaning of the biblical

message by analyzing the text. Commentaries come in single or double volumes that cover the whole Bible, as well as individual books that cover one book or passage of the Bible. There are three common types of commentaries:

a) Expository commentaries cover every verse and are good for help with interpreting a passage or verse.
b) Devotional commentaries read like a sermon and are good for devotions and daily application.
c) Homiletical commentaries deal with the text in outline form. They offer main themes, main points, and sub-points for the text you are studying.

BIBLE FACTS YOU SHOULD KNOW.

The Bible is...

A series of 66 books written by approximately 40 authors over a period of about 1,500 years. Yet the Bible stands as one book, unified by the theme of God and His relationship to man. In the 39 books of the Old Testament, we see the Lord working in and through a nation, Israel. In the 27 books of the New Testament, we see the Lord working in and through the Man, Jesus Christ.

God's revelation to His people. The word *revelation* means "unveiling." In Scripture, God has revealed divine truth. The Bible tells us all we need to know about who God is and what He requires of us. The Bible is a record of God's dealing with sinful humanity and His redeeming work to deliver individuals from sin. The dominant theme in the Bible is the Lord Jesus Christ, God's promised Savior.

The inspired Word of God. Theologian B.B. Warfield said, "The Bible is the Word of God in such a way that when the Bible speaks, God speaks." God gave the message of the Bible to the writers and prophets who, through human means, collected, recorded, accepted, authenticated, and handed down the Scriptures. As 2 Peter 1:21 says, "holy men of God spoke as they were moved by the Holy Spirit." The word *moved* is the same word used to describe the way a ship sails along under the power of a blowing wind. The biblical writers were moved by God to write what He wanted them to write.

Accurately passed down. The Law of Moses, or Pentateuch, was carefully maintained in the Hebrew community throughout the early centuries of its existence. As books continued to be written, they were safeguarded by priests and scribes. Ezra the scribe was instrumental in compiling many of the manuscripts that eventually came to be known as the Old Testament.

Trained scribes painstakingly copied the texts by hand. No word, letter, or mark could be written from memory. The scribe had to look directly at the original scroll for every stroke. Every letter, word, and verse of every book was counted and compared to the original.

The New Testament books were copied and shared by local Christian communities for several decades before being collected into the New Testament Canon. The New Testament Canon was identified by the early church and compiled by very strict and authentic criteria.

Verifiable as authentic. Fragments of the Old Testament, numbering in the tens of thousands, date back as far as the third century B.C. The Dead Sea Scrolls give us further evidence that the Old Testament was accurately maintained. New Testament manuscripts, numbering in the thousands, remain intact. No other writings of antiquity can be as carefully authenticated as the Bible.

Recommended Resources

Hendricks, Howard G., and William D. Hendricks. *Living by the Book.* Chicago, Ill.: Moody Publishing, 1991.

Lasseigne, Jeff. *Highway 66: A Unique Journey Through the 66 Books of the Bible.* Santa Ana, Calif.: Calvary Chapel Publishing, 2004.

Laurie, Greg. *New Believer's Guide to the Bible.* Wheaton, Ill.: Tyndale House, 2003.

grow

SALVATION AND YOUR CHRISTIAN WITNESS CHAPTER 2

ROOTED AND BUILT UP

As Christians, we have what a lost and indifferent world needs: the good news of salvation. Jesus Christ made a way for every person to be rescued from the sin that has left them damaged, empty and separated from God. Do you know anyone who could benefit from such good news? Have you told them what you know?

The apostle Paul was passionate about sharing the message of salvation with every person who would listen. Follow him through the book of Acts and you will see a man who was definitely not ashamed of the gospel! He took the message into synagogues where, as often as not, he was rejected. He took the message into the marketplace, where people listened politely and shrugged him off. He took the message to philosophers who found him amusing and to politicians who found him confusing.

He boldly shared the good news with unbelievers so they could be saved. He readily explained salvation to believers so they would fully understand the great gift they had been given.

Paul's lifelong passion to spread the gospel was deeply rooted in his own personal encounter with Jesus Christ. Knowing what God's saving power had done for him, Paul wasn't about to keep it to himself!

Can you relate? To be honest, many of us would probably say no. The thought of sharing our faith brings on the butterflies. We hesitate for fear of being rejected. We feel unskilled or, sadly, perhaps even unmotivated.

The aim of this chapter is to stir you up! The more we contemplate what this gift of salvation has accomplished in our own lives, the better equipped we will be to share the good news. Who knows? You may even discover that, like Paul, you are ready and eager to share the reason for the hope that is in you.

Salvation

God's Plan. The word *salvation* means "deliverance from the power and effects of sin." God knew we would sin and be separated from Him (see Romans 3:23) so He made a way for sinful people to be forgiven, made clean, and free to live in a loving relationship with Him (see Romans 5:8). The only way this could happen was for God's Son, Jesus Christ, to live a sinless human life and pay the penalty of sin with His own blood by dying on the cross. His death paid the price and His resurrection demonstrates the truth of His power over sin and death (see 1 Corinthians 15:3–4).

The Process. Are you an inquisitive person who likes to know how things fit together and work? For many, it's enough to know and accept that God has made a way of salvation through His Son. For those who wonder how it all happens, this chart will help you to appreciate each aspect of God's divine plan.

God's Sovereign Activity	The Individual's Response
Election/Predestination: Through grace, God chose salvation for those whom He knew would accept Him. He has a plan and purpose for their life (see Romans 8:29–30; Ephesians 1:4, 11; 2 Thessalonians 2:13).	**Belief:** Takes place when the truth of the gospel penetrates the heart of an individual (see Romans 10:9).
Regeneration: God makes us alive through Christ, enabling us to experience new birth (see 2 Corinthians 5:17; Ephesians 2:1, 4–5).	**Conviction:** Being keenly aware of one's sinful condition. The Holy Spirit brings this about in the heart of an unbeliever (see John 16:8).
Adoption: God gives us the full rights and privileges of inheritance in His family (see Galatians 4:4–6; Ephesians 1:5; Romans 8:15).	**Faith:** Firm confidence in the truth of God's Word that produces trust, hope, resolve and obedience (see Hebrews 11:1; 2 Timothy 1:12).
Sanctification: When we become Christians, God sets us apart for Himself, gradually and consistently developing the character of Christ in us as we yield ourselves to the work of the Holy Spirit (see 1 Corinthians 6:11; 2 Thessalonians 2:13; Philippians 1:6).	

The Power. Paul was not ashamed of the gospel because he knew from experience that Jesus has the power, or *dunamis*, to save a person and transform their life. This isn't the kind of power a person can possess. This isn't the kind of power that can be discovered in nature. This power is an inherent and inseparable characteristic of God's nature.

Think about what that means. Salvation is a powerful, life-transforming experience because it is God coming to live within you! We'll talk more about this in our chapter on the work of the Holy Spirit. For now, let the reality of what Christ has done for you sink in (see Ephesians 1:18–19).

Your Christian Witness

What does salvation produce? Paul stated it simply in 2 Corinthians 5:17 when he wrote, "Those who become Christians become new persons. They are not the same anymore, for the old life is gone. A new life has begun!" (NLT).

Some people have the idea that if they pray to receive Christ, He will cover their sins and they can continue living as they please. But salvation produces a changed life from the inside out. The evidence of our new life in Christ should be apparent to others and consistently increasing the longer we walk with the Lord. This is our Christian witness.

Sharing our faith must be a way of life that goes beyond words. In fact, it's possible to be skilled at telling people how to receive Christ and still be a very poor witness. So before we talk about witnessing with our words, let's consider some ways our life should be a powerful witness.

Witness with Your Life

Jesus said we should be "salt and light" to those around us (see Matthew 5:13–16). In simple terms, explain what that means.

_____

_____

As you read the following passages, list some of the ways we can be "salt and light."

John 13:34–35 _____

Galatians 5:22–23 _____

Philippians 2:14–15 _____

James 1:22–25 _____

Witness with Your Words

When Jesus commissioned believers to proclaim the good news (see Mark 16:15), He clearly meant we are to actively speak with unsaved people about the gospel. Many Christians take this command to heart, but don't know how to go about it.

Since there are a number of publications that give an excellent and thorough explanation (see the Recommended Resources listed at the end of this chapter for some suggested ones), we will focus on some basic reminders.

- *We are responsible to share the gospel, but only Jesus can save a person. Jesus said, "No one can come to Me unless the Father who sent Me draws him" (John 6:44).*

- *Depend on the Holy Spirit for courage and wisdom in what to say (see Acts 1:8; 1 Corinthians 2:1–5; 1 Thessalonians 1:5).*

- *Make sure your conversation stays centered on God's Word (see 2 Timothy 2:15; Ephesians 6:17; Hebrews 4:12).*

- *Pray! Pray while you prepare and pray while you share (see Colossians 4:2–3).*

Let's go back to a statement from the beginning of this session. Paul's lifelong passion to spread the gospel was deeply rooted in his own personal encounter with Jesus Christ. He knew what it was like to be a sinner whose life had been transformed by meeting Jesus.

Every Christian has a testimony of how Christ changed his or her life. You can use your testimony to reach out to an unsaved individual, letting them know you're someone they can relate to. Make your testimony brief and simple enough to be shared in a casual conversation that may only last a few minutes. The ability to do this takes some practice, so prepare your own "One-Minute Message" using the guidelines below.

1. **My Life Before Christ.** Don't glamorize your past, but mention what your life was like before Christ. Use simple words to describe how you felt, e.g., empty, hopeless, unhappy, self-centered.

2. **My Life Changed by Christ.** Summarize how you met Christ. Be sure to mention key elements of the gospel, even if you don't quote the verses. For example:
   I realized God loves me (see John 3:16).
   I knew I was a sinner (see Romans 3:23).
   I learned that Jesus died for me (see Romans 5:8).
   I wanted to turn my life around (see Acts 3:19).
   I asked Jesus to be part of my life (see Revelation 3:20).

3. **My New Life in Christ.** Tell how your life has changed. Use simple phrases that any person would understand, e.g., "I now have peace," "I've found a purpose in life," or "I've learned where to go for help with life's problems."

 grow

Use this space to write down your testimony. If possible, practice it with a partner and remember to keep it brief.

_____

_____

_____

_____

_____

_____

_____

_____

_____

_____

_____

TWELVE TIPS FOR EFFECTIVE WITNESSING*

1. Remember, your part is to share your faith, and it is God's part to convert the person (see John 6:44; John 16:7–11).

2. You may feel nervous about witnessing, but you can be sure the Holy Spirit will help you (see Acts 1:8). Depend on the Holy Spirit to work supernaturally. Pray! Before you talk to a person about God, talk to God about that person.

3. Don't look at people as projects. Don't just "zap" people with the gospel! These are precious individuals for whom Jesus Christ died. Ask God to give you a genuine concern for those you speak with.

4. As you witness, be friendly, pleasant, and positive (see Proverbs 12:18).

5. Avoid debating or arguing (see 2 Timothy 2:16, 23–26).

6. Avoid getting off the subject. If an individual gets off track with questions, even legitimate ones, assure them you will research the questions and give answers later. Then get back to the matter at hand, which is sharing the gospel.

7. Be sensitive. Do not shove the gospel into someone's face. Rather than trying to kick open a door, knock gently and rely on God to open the door of opportunity.

8. Use Scripture. God's Word will not return void, but your clever arguments won't be of lasting value (see Isaiah 55:11; Matthew 24:35; 2 Timothy 3:16–17).

9. Don't be afraid or embarrassed to say, "I don't know," when you are asked a question that you can't answer. Simply tell the person, "I don't know the answer, but I will try to find out for you."

10. Don't preach at people. Have a conversation with the other person. Ask questions, let them talk, listen to what they say, and respond appropriately.

11. Be yourself. Don't put on airs or try to come across in a way that makes you look super-spiritual.

12. If at all possible, bring the discussion to a point of decision. Ask the person if he or she would like to pray and receive Jesus Christ as Savior. We are sometimes afraid of being "pushy" while, in reality, the individual is wishing we would offer that opportunity.

* Adapted from Impact: *Equipping Believers to Impact Their World*

ESTABLISHED IN THE FAITH

Salvation and Your Christian Witness

The Good News

1. God loves us so much He made a way of salvation (see John 3:16, Romans 5:8).
2. Salvation comes through Jesus only (see John 10:9, Acts 4:12).
3. Salvation is a gracious gift of God (see Romans 6:23, Ephesians 2:8).
4. Salvation is offered to all who believe (see Acts 2:21, Romans 10:13).
5. Salvation brings peace with God (see Colossians 1:20–22, Romans 5:1,10).

> The woman at the well, after her soul-inspiring meeting with Jesus, left her waterpots, hurried into the city and tried to persuade others to come meet Him. "Come, see a man," she said, "which told me all things that ever I did: is not this the Christ?" Her excitement could not be contained within her own heart. She had to tell someone.
>
> —A.W. Tozer, The Set of The Sail.[3]

Sharing the Good News

1. Sharing the good news is a command (see Matthew 28:19–20, Mark 16:15).
2. God empowers and enables us to witness (see Acts 1:8, 2 Corinthians 3:4–5).
3. We should be prepared to witness (see 1 Peter 2:9, 2 Timothy 2:15, 4:2).
4. We witness with our words (see 1 Peter 2:9, 3:15; Colossians 4:6).
5. We witness with our life (see Matthew 5:13–16, Philippians 2:14–15).

Notes

 ABOUNDING

1. Can you think of one person whose witness, whether by their life or words, made an impression on you before you were saved? Share briefly how they influenced you.

2. For you, what is the most challenging part of witnessing? As you consider this, seek out suggestions that may ease your difficulty in this area.

3. Be prepared to share your "One-Minute Message."

Recommended Resources

Hold These Truths. Riverside, Calif.: Harvest Publications.

Impact: Equipping Believers to Impact Their World. Riverside, Calif.: Harvest Publications.

Laurie, Greg. *Four Keys to Effectively Share Your Faith,* Revised Edition. Riverside, Calif.: Harvest Publications, 2004.

Laurie, Greg. *New Believer's Guide to How to Share Your Faith.* Wheaton, Ill.: Tyndale House, 2002.

  grow

KNOWING GOD CHAPTER 3

MEMORY VERSE

*I will meditate on all Your work and muse on Your deeds.
Your way, O God, is holy; What god is great like our God?
Psalm 77:12–13 NASB*

ROOTED AND BUILT UP

Knowing God is the greatest pleasure and privilege there is in life. The man who penned Psalm 77 grasped this reality, declaring God's greatness to be a continual source of awe and wonder. A.W. Tozer once said that knowing God is the easiest and yet the most difficult thing in the world.

Coming to know God takes nothing more than believing with childlike faith (see Mark 10:15). At the same time, God is too great to be contained or fully explained.

When acute suffering compelled Job to cling to God, he thought about God's vast and magnificent power over all creation. From his humble mound of ashes, he declared all the wonders of God that a man can see and know to be "the mere edges of His ways, and how small a whisper we hear of Him!" (Job 26:14).

When the apostle Paul attempted, at length, to explain God's plan of redemption, his mind and heart reached a bursting point! "Oh the depth of riches," he wrote, "both of the wisdom and knowledge of God! How unsearchable are His judgments and His ways past finding out!" (Romans 11:33).

Have you ever turned the thought of God over and over in your mind? It is a healthy and humbling exercise.

As Christians, we must never stop seeking to know God better and love Him more. That is the aim of this session. If you will commit to meditate on the truth of Scripture, the Holy Spirit will give you eyes to see details of God's portrait that a passing glance can't fully appreciate.

Meditate on the Attributes of God

Some of God's attributes are essential qualities that He alone possesses. Knowing these attributes deepens our faith and stirs us to worship.

- God is **eternal.** While believers will live forever, only God is eternal. God was not created and there was never a time when He did not exist (see Psalm 90:2).

- God is **unchangeable.** The Bible teaches that God is *immutable*, which means He does not change. He has no need to develop further, and there is no danger that He will degenerate or become less than perfect in any way (see Psalm 102:25–27).

- God is **all-knowing.** The Bible teaches that God is *omniscient*, which means He has complete and perfect knowledge. God is fully aware at all times of all things and has unlimited understanding (see Psalm 139:1–6; Psalm 147:5).

- God is **ever-present.** The Bible teaches that God is *omnipresent*, which means He is present everywhere at all times. At the same time, God is not limited, nor can He be contained, by any space (see Jeremiah 23:24; 1 Kings 8:27).

- God is **all-powerful.** The Bible teaches that God is *omnipotent*, which means He has unlimited skill, strength, and ability to do all He desires to do. There is no challenge too difficult, no circumstance out of control, no problem beyond His ability to solve (see Jeremiah 32:27; Psalm 62:11) .

For personal reflection: How can being mindful of each of God's attributes increase your faith and help in your own prayer life?

_____

_____

_____

_____

Meditate on the Nature of God

> *"Hear, O Israel: The Lord our God, the Lord is One!"*
> *(Deuteronomy 6:4)*

The Bible clearly teaches that, within the nature of the one true God, there are three distinct and eternal persons: the Father, the Son, and the Holy Spirit. This is a mystery

  grow

the human mind can't fully penetrate, but the Bible plainly indicates there is no discrepancy in the teaching of the Trinity. Although the word *Trinity* is not found in the Bible, it is the best description of this biblical truth.

The most commonly used name for God in the Hebrew Old Testament is *Elohim*, which is plural. The repeated use of a plural term for the one true God (including the above mentioned Deuteronomy 6:4) gives us an Old Testament glimpse of the triune nature of God.

- God the **Father**. God is called the Father in both the Old and New Testaments. The Lord Himself said, "I am a Father to Israel . . . " (Jeremiah 31:9). Jesus called God "My Father" and taught the disciples to pray to "Our Father in heaven" (Matthew 6:9).

- God the **Son**. The Bible teaches that Jesus Christ is fully God and became a man. Jesus did not become God—He has always been God. Speaking of His participation in the creation of all things, the apostle John declares that Jesus existed before time began (see John 1:1–4). Jesus Himself said, "Before Abraham was, I AM" (John 8:58).

- God the **Holy Spirit**. Jesus told the disciples that when He returned to the Father, He would send "another Helper, that He may abide with you forever" (John 14:16). In Greek, the word another means "of the same kind." Jesus promised to send the Holy Spirit, who is distinct from, yet equal to, Jesus and His Father.

We worship a God who is far beyond what our minds can absorb or our language can explain. As the book of Isaiah tells us,

> "My thoughts are completely different from yours," says the Lord. "And my ways are far beyond anything you could imagine. For just as the heavens are higher than the earth, so are my ways higher than your ways and my thoughts higher than your thoughts." (Isaiah 55:8–9 NLT)

For personal reflection: Which of these diagrams helps you to better grasp the triune nature of God? Do your best to explain God's nature.

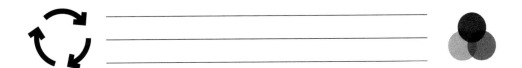

Meditate on the Character of God

As we have already seen, God has some essential qualities that He alone possesses. Now let's consider some of the characteristics of God that He gives us the capacity for also. These are qualities we can, and must, share with God. Jesus said, "You shall be perfect, just as your Father in heaven is perfect" (Matthew 5:48).

Before we look at these characteristics, we should be clear on two points:

First, because God is inherently perfect, He will always be infinitely more than we can ever imagine or hope to be. We can become wise, but God will always be infinitely wiser.

Some belief systems teach that humans can eventually become gods, but that does not line up with biblical truth in any way. The word *perfect* means "fully grown, mature." It gives the picture of having reached the goal for which every individual is intended, namely, to be a person who is conformed to the image of Christ (Romans 8:29).

Second, the only way these qualities are formed in us is by the power of the Holy Spirit's work in our lives. The Bible says, "As the Spirit of the Lord works within us, we become more and more like Him and reflect His glory even more" (2 Corinthians 3:18 NLT).

Simply put, our part is to read God's Word (which reveals who God is and what He is like) and then cooperate with the Holy Spirit, who will instruct us, convict us, and enable us to actively live out what we learn. The beauty of this process is that it isn't a long distance relationship. God's Holy Spirit lives *in* us, meaning we personally experience the benefits of God's character. We learn from first-hand encounters that God is loving, and so we understand how to love others.

So as you meditate on the character of God, know that He is all this and more for you and He will conform you to become more like Him in all your ways.

- God is **holy**. The Greek word for holy (*hosios*) means "unpolluted with wickedness." God is completely "set apart"—as the Hebrew text defines holy— from all that is evil, impure, or depraved. He has no part with sin (see Habakkuk 1:13). God's holiness is the standard, the pattern for His people to emulate. As individuals, we must be morally, ethically, spiritually, and physically pure.

- God is **righteous** and **just**. God always does what is right and fair. God Himself is the definition of what is right and He is fair in all His dealings with humanity. Because He is righteous, God requires obedience and trust—even when we can't see or understand what He is doing. Because God is just, He will not allow sin to go unpunished, or injustice to prevail. We all struggle with the reality that "life isn't

  grow

fair." We need to remember, as the apostle Paul said in Romans 9:22, that "God has every right to exercise His judgment and His power" (NLT). We can know with certainty that the day will come when we will understand and praise God for His ways (see Revelation 15:3–4).

- God is **loving.** One simple definition of God's love is that He "eternally gives of Himself to others." Let the magnitude of that sink in. God's love is unconditional and cannot be earned or lost. In spite of our unlovable condition (see Romans 5:7–8), God chose to love us. His love exceeds our comprehension (see Ephesians 3:19) and compels us to love Him in return (Jeremiah 31:3).

- God is **merciful** and **gracious.** God is moved with compassion toward those who suffer, whether by circumstances out of their control or even through misery brought on by their own sinfulness. In mercy, He relieves our pain and pardons our sin (see Psalm 103:8–14). In grace, He covers our sin with His own blood and saves us from the punishment we deserve (see Romans 3:24; Ephesians 2:8–9). Just as the apostle Paul attributed his life and service to God's grace (see 1 Corinthians 15:10), we can depend on God to give us all we need to live for and serve Him (see 2 Corinthians 9:8; 12:9).

- God is **faithful.** God is completely trustworthy and true to His Word. He can be relied on and will always do what He has promised (see Numbers 23:19). As His servants, we are expected by God to be faithful, and He will reward us accordingly (see Matthew 25:14–29).

For personal reflection: Which of these godly characteristics would you say you have shown the most growth in? Which would you say you have farthest yet to go?

_____

_____

_____

_____

_____

_____

_____

_____

_____

_____

_____

ESTABLISHED IN THE FAITH

> *An unknown God can neither be trusted, served, nor worshipped…Something more than a theoretical knowledge of God is needed by us. God is only truly known in the soul as we yield ourselves to Him, submit to His authority, and regulate all the details of our lives by His holy precepts and commandments.*
>
> —A.W. Pink, The Attributes of God.[4]

Knowing God

God's Attributes

1. God is eternal (see Psalm 90:2; Revelation 1:8).
2. God is unchangeable (see Psalm 102:25–27; Hebrews 13:8).
3. God is all-knowing (see Job 34:21; Hebrews 4:13).
4. God is ever-present (see Psalm 139:7–12; Jeremiah 23:24).
5. God is all-powerful (see Jeremiah 32:27; Psalm 62:11).

God's Nature

1. There is only one true God (see Deuteronomy 4:35; Isaiah 44:6–8).
2. One God, Three Persons:
   a) God the Father (see Isaiah 64:8; Matthew 6:9).
   b) God the Son (see John 1:1–4; John 8:58; Philippians 2:5–7).
   c) God the Spirit (see John 4:24; John 14:16; 2 Corinthians 3:17).

God's Character

1. God is holy (see Psalm 99:9; Isaiah 6:3; Revelation 15:4).
2. God is righteous (see Psalm 119:137; Psalm 145:17).
3. God is just (see Zephaniah 3:5; John 5:30; Revelation 15:3).
4. God is loving (see Jeremiah 31:3; Ephesians 2:4; 1 John 3:1).
5. God is merciful (see 2 Samuel 22:26; Psalm 36:5; Psalm 103:11).
6. God is gracious (see Psalm 84:11; Ephesians 2:7; Titus 2:11).
7. God is faithful (see Psalm 36:5; 1 Corinthians 1:9; 2 Timothy 2:13).

Notes

_____

_____

_____

_____

_____

_____

_____

_____

_____

_____

_____

_____

_____

_____

_____

_____

_____

_____

_____

_____

_____

_____

_____

ABOUNDING

1. Recite Psalm 77:12–13. Think of one aspect of God's character that stirs a sense of awe within you.

2. In practical terms, how do you relate to God as the Father, as the Son, and as the Holy Spirit?

3. For you personally, what has been the most instructive part of this chapter on knowing God?

Recommended Resources

Grudem, Wayne. *Systematic Theology.* Grand Rapids, Mich.: Zondervan Publishing, 1994.

Hold These Truths. Riverside, Calif.: Harvest Publications.

Pink, A.W. *The Attributes of God.* Grand Rapids, Mich.: Baker Books, 1991.

Tozer, A.W. *Knowledge of the Holy.* New York: HarperCollins, 1998.

  grow

THE WORK OF THE HOLY SPIRIT CHAPTER 4

ROOTED AND BUILT UP

Jesus called the Holy Spirit "the Helper." When you think of a helper, what comes to mind? You might picture a person who assists you in accomplishing a task. Or maybe you think of a tool—some inanimate object that becomes useful in your hands.

While the first description comes close, neither explanation sufficiently describes the work of the Holy Spirit in our life. Since the Holy Spirit is God, He is the senior partner in this working relationship and we must get to know Him with the intention of following His lead. Our aim should not be *how can I get more of the Holy Spirit*, but rather, *how can the Holy Spirit have more of me?*

With, In, Upon

Jesus promised to send the Holy Spirit, who would be *with* and *live* in the disciples (see John 14:16–17). In the original language, the word for *with* describes a close companion who lives among, or in the midst of, God's people. We can think of this as the Spirit's unifying presence in the body of believers that comprises the Church (see Ephesians 4:4–6).

But the Holy Spirit also works personally and individually in the life of every believer. When you accepted Jesus as your Savior and Lord, the Holy Spirit came to live and work *in* you (see 1 Corinthians 12:13, 1 Corinthians 6:19).

- He made you spiritually alive (see John 3:5; 6:63).
- His presence is God's "seal" that you belong to Him (see Ephesians 1:13–14).
- He is your constant companion, teacher, and guide (see John 14:26; 16:13).
- His presence enables you to have victory over sin (see Romans 8:11; 6:14).

Because the Holy Spirit lives *in* you, He works from the inside out to make you more like Christ. Through salvation, Jesus has made this new life possible. Through sanctification, the Holy Spirit makes this new life practical.

For this, He needs our cooperation. We need to put aside our old ways of thinking and acting and then start to walk in the Spirit. How do we, in real life ways, begin walking in the Spirit?

God's Word gives us a map to follow. Read Colossians 3:8–10 and write down what we are to put off. Then read verses 12–14 and list what we are to put on.

Put Off...	Put On...

Looking at this list, you may be thinking, "I don't know if I can do that! Maybe for a day or a week—a month if I try really hard. But sooner or later, I'm going to fail. Does that mean I'm not walking in the Spirit?" That's a good question, so let's get this matter settled. When you became a Christian, the Holy Spirit took up residence in your life and gave you a new nature (see Romans 8:9). The Holy Spirit's "house rules" state that "Sin shall not be master over you, for you are not under law, but under grace" (Romans 6:14 NASB).

This creates a conflict between your old nature and your new nature (which, by the way, you will always have this side of heaven). Every time your old sinful nature tries to take control, you can choose to give in or point to the "house rules" and depend on the Holy Spirit to back you up.

Walking in the Spirit means that you recognize that you are powerless to change on your own and so you rely on the Holy Spirit to overcome the sinful urges. His power was great enough to raise Jesus from the dead (see Romans 8:11), so there is no battle He cannot help you win. The key to victory is your cooperation.

> *In the Spirit's power it is our privilege to get daily, hourly, constant victory over the flesh and over sin. This victory is not in ourselves, nor in any strength of our own.*
>
> —*R.A. Torrey, The Person and Work of the Holy Spirit.*[5]

 grow

While the Holy Spirit works in us, He also works through us. As followers of Jesus, we are called to serve Him. But in order to do God's work, we need the power of the Holy Spirit to come upon us. This is known as the baptism of the Holy Spirit.

After Jesus' resurrection, He instructed the disciples not to begin the work He called them to do until they were baptized in the Holy Spirit (see Luke 24:49; Acts 1:4,8). Here were men who had walked and worked with Jesus through His earthly life and ministry, yet they needed something more. Jesus said, "But you will receive power when the Holy Spirit has come upon you; and you shall be My witnesses . . . " (Acts 1:8).

Why do we need the baptism of the Holy Spirit?

The baptism of the Holy Spirit empowers believers to be bold in their witness and personal testimony, and to effectively do the work God gives them. When the Holy Spirit comes upon a believer, he or she receives power for service and spiritual gifts for the purpose of proclaiming the gospel and strengthening the body of Christ.

When does the baptism of the Holy Spirit happen?

The baptism of the Holy Spirit is distinct from, and in addition to, the initial indwelling of God's Spirit in our heart at salvation. However, some believers do receive the baptism of the Holy Spirit at the moment of conversion. Read the following scriptures and note when the baptism of the Holy Spirit happened.

	At Conversion	After Conversion
Believers in Samaria (Acts 8:14–16)	☐	☐
Cornelius and his family (Acts 10:43–48)	☐	☐
Ephesian believers (Acts 19:1–6)	☐	☐

Do we need the baptism of the Holy Spirit more than once?

Technically, the answer is no; but since the term is frequently used in more than one sense, we should explain. The expression *baptism* is never used in Scripture to describe subsequent fillings. Peter himself used it to describe an introductory experience in Acts 11:15 when he said, "And as I began to speak, the Holy Spirit fell upon them, as upon us at the beginning." In this sense, we need to be baptized in the Holy Spirit only once, just as salvation and water baptism need only occur one time.

On the other hand, "filled with the Holy Spirit" is the phrase used in Acts 2:4 to describe what happened when the promise of Acts 1:5 was fulfilled. And the New Testament clearly teaches the need for repeated fillings. In Ephesians 5:18, Paul commands believers to be (literally, "be being") filled with the Spirit.

As believers seeking to glorify God and serve Him to the utmost capacity, we need to ask the Lord daily to fill us with His Holy Spirit. Without the power of the Holy Spirit, we can't effectively serve the Lord for one day any more than we can expect to hold our breath for one hour!

OPTIONAL DISCOVERY EXERCISE:
How many names can you find for the Holy Spirit?

Hebrews 9:14 _____   1 Peter 4:14 _____   Isaiah 11:2 _____

Luke 1:35 _____   Romans 1:4 _____   Romans 8:2 _____

Romans 8:15 _____   Isaiah 4:4 _____   John 14:17 _____

How do we receive the baptism of the Holy Spirit?

Jesus said, "If you then, being evil, know how to give good gifts to your children, how much more will your heavenly Father give the Holy Spirit to those who ask Him!" (Luke 11:13)

As a believer who genuinely desires to give yourself wholly to God in love and service, you need only ask and believe God to fulfill His promise. When you ask for something according to God's will, you can be confident He will answer (see 1 John 5:14–15).

Have you asked?

ESTABLISHED IN THE FAITH

> The Spirit-filled life is not a special, deluxe edition of Christianity. It is part and parcel of the total plan of God for His people.
>
> —A.W. Tozer, The Best of A.W. Tozer.[6]

The Work of the Holy Spirit

In the World

1. The Holy Spirit convicts people of the sin of unbelief (see John 16:8–11).
2. The Holy Spirit leads people to salvation through Jesus (see 1 Corinthians 12:3).
3. The Holy Spirit restrains the spread of evil (see 2 Thessalonians 2:7).

In the Believer

1. The Holy Spirit indwells the believer (see John 14:16–17; 1 Corinthians 3:16).
2. The Holy Spirit assures the believer of salvation (see Romans 8:16; 1 John 5:7,10–11).
3. The Holy Spirit regenerates the believer (see John 6:63; Romans 8:11; Titus 3:4–7).
4. The Holy Spirit instructs and guides the believer (see John 14:26; John 16:13).
5. The Holy Spirit enables the believer to obey (see Ezekiel 36:27).
6. The Holy Spirit helps the believer to pray (see Romans 8:26–27).
7. The Holy Spirit enlightens the believer (see 1 Corinthians 2:12–14).
8. The Holy Spirit empowers the believer (see Acts 1:8; 1 Corinthians 2:4; Ephesians 3:16).

Notes

_____

_____

_____

_____

_____

_____

_____

_____

_____

_____

_____

_____

_____

_____

 ABOUNDING

1. Consider the statement in the opening paragraph of this chapter: "Our aim should not be *how can I get more of the Holy Spirit*, but rather, *how can the Holy Spirit have more of me?*" How would you answer that statement?

2. Give three specific examples of how the Holy Spirit is a helper for believers.

3. What is the primary purpose for the baptism of the Holy Spirit?

Recommended Resources

Laurie, Greg. *A Passion for God*. Eugene, Ore.: Harvest House Publishers, 1998.

Lloyd-Jones, Martyn. *Joy Unspeakable*. Wheaton, Ill.: Harold Shaw Publishers, 1985.

Smith, Chuck. *Charisma vs. Charismania*. Costa Mesa, Calif.: The Word For Today Publishers, 2000.

Torrey, R.A. *The Person and Work of the Holy Spirit*. Grand Rapids, Mich.: Zondervan Publishing, 1985.

  grow

THE GIFTS OF THE HOLY SPIRIT CHAPTER 5

ROOTED AND BUILT UP

As members of the body of Christ, we are called to a life of service. Do you want to have an impact, being a godly influence in the lives of the people God brings across your path? You can, you know. God designed you for good works (see Ephesians 2:10). All the natural talents and abilities you possess (and devote so much time and effort to develop) are a gift from Him.

But wait, there's more! God also gives spiritual gifts to His children to be used for His purpose and pleasure. You have something to contribute and it's up to you to discover and develop that spiritual gift. We're here to help, so let's get started.

Unity and Diversity

The Bible specifically discusses the gifts of the Holy Spirit in three passages: Romans 12:3–8; 1 Corinthians 12:4–12, 27–31; and Ephesians 4:11–16. In each passage, we see unity (one body) and diversity (individual gifts). God designed the church to be a healthy body, with each member performing a unique function while all the parts work together.

This unity is due to the powerful presence of the Holy Spirit. He does the work and gives at least one gift to every believer according to His perfect will. We should be faithful to seek what gifts we've been given and use them for God's glory. Before looking at each gift individually, let's consider three essential truths about all spiritual gifts.

Characteristics of Spiritual Gifts

When Paul wrote to the Corinthians about spiritual gifts, he used three specific words in his opening thoughts. Careful examination of each word helps us to understand and appreciate a particular aspect of the gifts of the Holy Spirit.

1. **Grace gifts.** "There are diversities of gifts, but the same Spirit" (1 Corinthians 12:4). The word for gifts is *charismata*, meaning "manifestations of grace." By this, we understand that spiritual gifts are an undeserved benefit of Christian life. God graciously gives what we need and He alone is the source of power. We cannot take credit for the gifts, nor can we decide which gifts we are given.

2. **Ministry gifts.** "There are differences of ministries, but the same Lord" (1 Corinthians 12:5). The word for ministries is *diakoniai*, meaning "service that benefits others." By this, we understand that spiritual gifts are for the good of the whole church. Paul restates this in Ephesians 4:12 by saying spiritual gifts are "for the equipping of the saints for the work of ministry." They are not given for personal fulfillment or selfish use.

3. **Active gifts.** "There are diversities of activities, but it is the same God who works all in all" (1 Corinthians 12:6). The word for activities is *energemata*, meaning "the resulting effects of energy." By this, we understand that spiritual gifts are meant to be exercised. We must be obedient to put the gifts to work, trusting God to energize our efforts to accomplish His purpose.

Description of Spiritual Gifts

Before looking at a description of spiritual gifts, let's consider what the gifts of the Spirit are not. First, the gifts of the Spirit are not the same as the fruit of the Spirit. The fruit of the Spirit (Galatians 5:22–23) is produced by God working *in* us to make us more like Christ. As we obey and abide (see John 15:4), the Holy Spirit shapes our character. God wants all believers to bear *every* fruit of the Spirit.

I believe the discovery of our spiritual gifts should be a matter of careful and thoughtful prayer on our part. Also we should be sure we are willing to make use of our spiritual gifts in a way that is honoring to God.

Whether the Holy Spirit gives us one or several, it is important for us to do two things: First, we should recognize the gift or gifts God has given us. Second, we should nurture those gifts and do everything, humanly speaking, to improve them as we use them.

—Billy Graham, The Holy Spirit: Activating God's Power in Your Life.[7]

  grow

Second, spiritual gifts are not the same as our spiritual responsibilities. For example, a person may not have the gift of an evangelist, but every believer is called to share the gospel (see Matthew 28:19–20). All do not receive the gift of wisdom, but every believer is instructed to conduct themselves with wisdom (see Colossians 4:5). It is up to the Spirit to impart the gift of generous giving, but we are all expected to give with a willing and cheerful heart (see 2 Corinthians 9:7). To some, the Spirit gives a supernatural measure of faith, but every believer is called to walk by faith (see 2 Corinthians 5:7).

According to Romans 12:6, each believer has at least one spiritual gift to be used for the benefit of the body and to the glory of God. Perhaps you have already discovered your spiritual gift(s). If you have, how are you putting it or them to use?

_____

_____

_____

_____

_____

_____

Many believers are not using their gifts because they haven't identified them. The process of recognizing your gift(s) may take some time, but don't get discouraged. Here are some helpful guidelines:

- **Understand.** Recognizing your gift begins with understanding what the Bible says about spiritual gifts. The aim of this chapter is to help you get a solid biblical understanding of each gift and how it works.

- **Ask.** We are urged to ask for spiritual gifts (Luke 11:13; 1 Corinthians 12:31).

- **Know.** Part of discovering your spiritual gift(s) involves knowing yourself. What area of service do you lean toward? It may be that what you recognize as a natural talent is a God-given desire that the Holy Spirit is waiting for you to offer wholeheartedly to Him.

- **Practice.** Start serving! If you have a spiritual gift in that area, it will begin to show itself in productive results. You may not see it initially, but other Christians will confirm that gift by expressing blessings or asking you to use your gift in ministry.

Here is a summary of spiritual gifts listed in Romans, 1 Corinthians, and Ephesians:

Gift	Description	Example
Prophecy Romans 12:6; 1 Corinthians 12:28	The capacity to proclaim and apply God's truth and expose sin.	Acts 11:27–28; Acts 15:32; 1 Corinthians 14:3–5
Service/Helps/Hospitality Romans 12:7; 1 Corinthians 12:28	The capacity to assist others in practical ways, freeing them to fulfill their own calling.	Acts 6:1–7; 2 Timothy 1:16; 1 Peter 4:11
Teaching Romans 12:7; 1 Corinthians 12:28; Ephesians 4:11	The capacity to educate by clearly explaining and applying God's Word.	Acts 18:11, 24–28; Titus 2:3
Encouragement Romans 12:8	The capacity to comfort and encourage in a way that stimulates the hearer to act on God's Word.	Acts 14:22; Hebrews 10:24; 1 Thessalonians 2:11–12
Giving Romans 12:8	The capacity to generously and cheerfully contribute material resources for the work of the Lord.	Mark 12:41–44; 2 Corinthians 8:1–5
Leadership/Administration Romans 12:8; 1 Corinthians 12:28	The capacity to instill vision, motivate people, and manage resources to accomplish ministry.	Acts 6:1–7; 1 Timothy 3; Hebrews 13:7, 17
Mercy Romans 12:8	The capacity to detect hurt and respond with acts of compassion toward those who are hurting.	Acts 9:26–27; Luke 10:30–37
Apostle 1 Corinthians 12:29; Ephesians 4:11	Meaning "sent one", the capacity to start new ministries and oversee their development. (This is not the same as the New Testament's designation of the 12 apostles.)	Acts 13:1-4; Romans 15:20
Evangelist Ephesians 4:11	The capacity to present the gospel with great clarity and effectiveness.	Acts 8:5–6, 26–40
Pastor/Teacher (Shepherd) Ephesians 4:11	The capacity to guide and nurture others to grow in faith.	1 Peter 5:1-4; Acts 20:28; 1 Thessalonians 2:7–12
Word of Wisdom 1 Corinthians 12:8	A word of wisdom is when God (having complete knowledge of past, present, and future) reveals His plan or will in a certain matter to man in a specific time of need.	Acts 15:13–21; Luke 21:12–15; 1 Thessalonians 4:15–18
Word of Knowledge 1 Corinthians 12:8	Knowledge concerning a person or situation not acquired through natural means, but revealed by the Holy Spirit.	Acts 9:10–12, 15–16; 2 Kings 6:8–12
Faith 1 Corinthians 12:9	The capacity to believe and obey God for things outside the realm of normal faith.	Romans 4:18–21; Hebrews 11
Healing 1 Corinthians 12:9	The capacity to exercise the healing power that comes from God and is given solely according to His will.	Acts 3:1–10; Acts 9:32–34; Acts 20:9–12
Miracles 1 Corinthians 12:10	When God works outside the realm of natural law, it is a miracle. When He uses a believer to do this, it is the working of miracles.	Exodus 17; 2 Kings 6:1–7; Acts 9:36–41; Acts 13:8–12
Discernment 1 Corinthians 12:10	The capacity to distinguish whether the source of an act or a teaching is divine, human, or evil.	Matthew 16:21–23; Acts 8:18–23; Acts 13:9–10
Tongues 1 Corinthians 12:10	The capacity to speak praises to God in an unknown language. This can be used in prayer life for personal edification. Tongues are not given to every believer as evidence they have received baptism of the Holy Spirit.	Acts 2:4–11; Acts 10:44–46
Interpretation of Tongues 1 Corinthians 12:10	The capacity to interpret what is spoken in tongues. This will always be praise to God and not a message to people. The gift of tongues is not to be publicly used unless one who interprets is present.	1 Corinthians 14:2,6–13,27–28

ESTABLISHED IN THE FAITH

> *Attaining spiritual gifts is not the goal—they are the gateway. They are not a hobby to play with—they are tools to build with, weapons to fight with. We will be more effective as we put them to use for God's glory and not our own.*
>
> —Greg Laurie, New Believer's Bible New Testament.[8]

Spiritual Gifts

Characteristics and Purpose

1. Given by God's grace for the purpose of effective service (see 1 Corinthians 12:4–6).
2. Spiritual gifts build up the body of Christ (see 1 Corinthians 12:7).
3. Spiritual gifts are different than spiritual fruit (see Galatians 5:22–23).
4. There are a variety of gifts, but unity of purpose (see Romans 12:4–5).
5. The Holy Spirit determines which gifts to give us (see 1 Corinthians 12:11).

Use and Misuse

1. We have a responsibility to discover and develop our gifts (see Romans 12:6).
2. We must use our gifts to serve others (see 1 Peter 4:10; Philippians 2:3–4).
3. We must not neglect to use our gifts (see 2 Timothy 1:6; Matthew 25:23).
4. We must not take pride in, or demean, our gift (see 1 Corinthians 12:14–26).
5. Gifts should not be used in a way that is divisive or disruptive (see 1 Corinthians 14).
6. Proper use of gifts will result in maturity, stability, unity and a healthy church! (see Ephesians 4:11–16)

Notes

_____

_____

_____

_____

_____

_____

_____

_____

_____

_____

_____

_____

 ABOUNDING

1. How have you benefited from someone else exercising their spiritual gift(s)? Give at least two examples.

2. To the best of your understanding, what spiritual gift(s) do you have? How are you using each gift to serve the Lord and others?

3. For you personally, what would help you to better understand and/or effectively use your spiritual gift(s)? Try to be brief and specific.

Recommended Resources

Graham, Billy. _The Holy Spirit: Activating God's Power in Your Life._ Nashville, Tenn.: W Publishing Group, 2000.

Laurie, Greg. _A Passion for God._ Eugene, Ore.: Harvest House Publishers, 1998.

Lloyd-Jones, Martyn. _Joy Unspeakable._ Wheaton, Ill.: Harold Shaw Publishers, 1985.

Smith, Chuck. _Charisma vs. Charismania._ Costa Mesa, Calif.: The Word For Today Publishers, 2000.

Torrey, R.A. _The Person and Work of the Holy Spirit._ Grand Rapids, Mich.: Zondervan Publishing, 1985.

SPIRITUAL WARFARE CHAPTER 6

ROOTED AND BUILT UP

When you became a Christian, some amazing changes took place. God canceled your debt of sin and credited the righteousness of Jesus into your account. Your heart became Christ's home, so extensive repairs and renovations are underway!

You have been given full rights and family access as a child of God. You are free to come to your Heavenly Father at all times, knowing He welcomes you with open arms and a heart full of love.

Another change took place the moment you asked Jesus to be your Savior and Lord. The devil sees you differently now. Before, you were just another hopeless human. Now you're the enemy. And the war is on.

Writing to the Corinthians, Paul made certain they were aware of the invisible war they were engaged in. "For though we walk in the flesh," he told them, "we do not war according to the flesh, for the weapons of our warfare are not of the flesh, but divinely powerful for the destruction of fortresses" (2 Corinthians 10:3–4 NASB). In plain terms, the Christian life is a battleground.

Frankly, the devil wants you to be a living, breathing casualty of war, without you even realizing it. But God has equipped us for battle, and even revealed the enemy's strategy. What's more, we already know what the outcome will be! "But thanks be to God, who gives us the victory through our Lord Jesus Christ" (1 Corinthians 15:57).

In this chapter, we will trace out the enemy's tactics and focus in on the resources God has given us to resist, stand firm, and gain ground in this spiritual battle.

Wartime Propaganda

Out of our 21st-century cyberspace world comes a new term: information warfare. It is the attempt to disrupt, exploit, and corrupt an enemy's computers, networking systems, and every form of information in order to achieve an advantage. A hacker gets into an important system and spreads a virus. Information is stolen, re-routed, and misused for damaging purposes. Although the technology is new, the tactic is ancient, dating back to the Garden of Eden.

When Satan approached Eve, he smoothly engaged her in a conversation about what God had said (Genesis 3:1–7). He got her to question God's Word, denied God's Word, and ultimately corrupted her mind by substituting his own lie. It was such a simple and effective strategy that it became his primary weapon.

The devil has built up such an arsenal of lies that, humanly speaking, he appears unbeatable. As 2 Corinthians 10:4 says, the world is his *stronghold* (NKJV). That word can be translated as "a strongly fortified place where a group, having certain views and attitudes is heavily concentrated."

The apostle Paul didn't just urge believers to pull down strongholds. He identified two specific areas where the battle gets particularly fierce (see 2 Corinthians 10:5). In a physical war, the fiercest combat takes place on the frontlines. In spiritual warfare, the frontlines are never "over there" as though they can be escaped or avoided. To locate the frontlines of a spiritual battle, we need only look into our hearts and minds.

"Casting down arguments . . . " Arguments (*logismos*) speak of ideas, reasoning, and mental calculations that lead up to and determine conduct. Paul uses the word here in reference to attitudes and/or ideas that are hostile to the gospel. Simply put, the argument is *you don't really need God—do it your way.* Eve heard it first in the garden and this spiritual virus has been wreaking havoc ever since.

"Every high thing that exalts itself . . . " Every high thing (*hupsoma*) refers to a thing that has been elevated to the point of becoming a barrier. In this verse, Paul uses it to refer to opinions or attitudes that create a barrier, preventing an individual from having personal experience with, and true knowledge of, God.

> *"Satan, the god of this evil world, has blinded the minds of those who don't believe, so they are unable to see the glorious light of the Good News that is shining upon them"* (2 Corinthians 4:4 NLT).

The devil's strategy is to keep people spiritually blind so they will die in their sins. For unbelievers, this tactic is lethal but vigilance is needed among Christians as well. If we cling to any part of a worldly mindset, we will suffer collateral damage (see Romans 12:1–2).

In this invisible battle for hearts and minds, spiritual armor isn't just helpful or desirable, it is vital. Are you wearing your spiritual armor?

Weapons of our Warfare

Ephesians 6:11 tells us to "Put on the whole armor of God, so that you might be able to stand against the wiles of the devil." God doesn't want us to go into battle ill-equipped. But if we don't understand the purpose behind a piece of armor, we might foolishly leave it behind! As you read about the armor God has provided, think of the purpose it serves and why you need it. Keep your answers brief and practical.

A Soldier's Equipment	Armor of God	Purpose in Spiritual Battle
Girdle – A leather apron cinched at the waist. Gives protection and provides mobility. Also used as a sheath for the soldier's sword.	Truth Psalm 51:6; John 17:17; Proverbs 23:23	
Breastplate – Body armor that covers a soldier's front and back, protecting vital organs.	Righteousness Philippians 3:9; 1 Timothy 6:11	
Shoes – Leather sandals with nails in the soles for firm footing; enabling a soldier to travel over rocky or uneven terrain without falling.	Gospel of Peace Romans 5:1–2; Isaiah 52:7	
Shield – Large enough for a soldier to hide behind. Made of wood and leather; often dipped in water so fire arrows could not damage it.	Faith Hebrews 11:1; 1 John 5:4–5	
Helmet – Because the head is a vulnerable target, a soldier never goes into battle without his helmet.	Salvation 2 Peter 3:18; Philippians 4:8; 2 Corinthians 11:3	
Sword – Offensive weapon used to defend the soldier and attack his enemy.	Word of God Hebrews 4:12; 2 Timothy 2:15; 2 Timothy 3:16–17	
Prayer – Paul made it clear that prayer is a partner to the Word of God. You might say that prayer gives us power to hold up the sword of God's Word in a spiritual battle.	Prayer Ephesians 6:18; Philippians 4:6–7; Colossians 4:2; 1 Thessalonians 5:16–18	

Wage the Battle

Feeling shell-shocked? Battle weary? Sometimes it feels like we're losing the struggle against sin—even the apostle Paul felt that way at times (see Romans 7:18–24).

Hang in there. Keep your eyes on Jesus who "endured such hostility by sinners against Himself, so that you will not grow weary and lose heart" (Hebrews 12:3 NASB).

Jesus gave us the same resources He used to overcome the enemy. When He was tempted, He used the Word of God. As a man, He experienced the same weaknesses we face and overcame them by the indwelling power of the Holy Spirit. Now He sits at the right hand of God, interceding for you (see Hebrews 7:25). Think about that. He is interceding for you. How can you lose?

> *"I have given them Your word; and the world has hated them, because they are not of the world. . . . I do not ask You to take them out of the world, but to keep them from the evil one. They are not of the world, even as I am not of the world. Sanctify them in the truth; Your Word is truth." (John 17:14-17 NASB)*

ESTABLISHED IN THE FAITH

The Spirit-filled life is not, as many suppose, a life of peace and quiet pleasure. It is likely something quite the opposite. ...If we want to escape the struggle we have but to draw back... that is all Satan wants. Compromise will take the pressure off. Satan will not bother a man who has quit fighting. But the cost of quitting will be a life of peaceful stagnation. We sons of eternity just cannot afford such a thing.

—A.W. Tozer, That Incredible Christian.[9]

Spiritual Warfare

Our Battle

1. Our battle is spiritual in nature (see 2 Corinthians 10:3–5).
2. Our strength comes from God (see Ephesians 6:10; 1 John 5:18).
3. Victory is assured (see Colossians 2:15; 1 Corinthians 15:57).

Our Enemies

1. The World (see 1 John 2:15–16).
2. The Flesh (see Romans 7:18–23).
3. The Devil (see 1 Peter 5:8; Revelation 12:10).

Our Enemies

1. Our weapons are spiritually powerful (see 2 Corinthians 10:4).
2. Our armor is the light (see Romans 13:12).
3. The armor of God (see Ephesians 6:14–18).

Notes

_____
_____
_____
_____
_____
_____
_____
_____
_____
_____
_____
_____
_____
_____
_____
_____
_____
_____
_____
_____
_____
_____
_____
_____

ABOUNDING

1. Recite Ephesians 6:10. Is this a command only for the times when we're consciously engaged in a spiritual battle? Why, or why not?

2. Generally speaking, what are some areas where Christians today might be particularly vulnerable to a worldly mindset? What practical steps can we take to guard ourselves?

3. For you personally, what has been the most helpful or eye-opening part of this chapter?

Recommended Resources

Laurie, Greg. *What the Devil Doesn't Want You to Know*, Revised Edition. Riverside, Calif.: Harvest Publications, 2004.

Tozer, A.W. *That Incredible Christian.* Camp Hill, Pa.: Christian Publications, 1986.

Wiersbe, Warren. *The Strategy of Satan.* Wheaton, Ill.: Tyndale House, 1979.

Wiersbe, Warren. *What to Wear to the War.* Lincoln, Neb.: Back to the Bible Publishing, 1986.

Wilson, Jim. *Principles of War: A Handbook on Strategic Evangelism.* Moscow, Idaho: Community Christian Ministries. http://www.ccmbooks.org/onlinebooks/pow/index.htm

 grow

MEMORY VERSE

But the end of all things is at hand; therefore be serious and watchful in your prayers.
1 Peter 4:7

ROOTED AND BUILT UP

"It's time."

Two simple words with the power to summon up a whole range of emotions. A sentimental whisper from a father as he walks his daughter down the aisle. For the one awaiting test results, it's the cautious announcement that the doctor will see you now. To a death row inmate, it signals the end of the line. Uttered by an expectant mother, those words send a leap of excitement and wonder into motion.

Imagine what it will be like when the one saying, "It's time," is Jesus Christ, our returning Lord and King!

While no one knows the day or time of Christ's return, Jesus tells us to be ready. As believers, we can look forward to Jesus' imminent return with confidence because the Bible says so. The Bible is the only book that can reveal the future with 100 percent accuracy.

As it says in the book of Isaiah, "For I am God, and there is no other; I am God, and there is none like Me, declaring the end from the beginning. And from ancient times things that are not yet done, saying, 'My counsel shall stand, and I will do all My pleasure'" (Isaiah 46:9–10).

All of the prophecies concerning the first coming of Jesus (more than one hundred) were fulfilled exactly as foretold. There is no legitimate reason, then, to question whether the prophecies of last days events and the Lord's second coming will also happen as predicted.

That is not to say, however, that we don't have questions. Many Christians shy away from studying last days events because they feel it is too complex and mysterious to understand. But Jesus said we must learn to read the signs of the times (see Luke 21:29–31). Why? So we will be diligent to live faithfully in the present while we look forward with hope to Christ's return, whenever that may be.

In this session, we will look at several key events that lead to the final chapter of world history, and end with a glimpse into eternity.

Ready for His Return

The rapture is the biblical teaching that Jesus will come for His church. At the appointed time, all living Christians will be *caught up* ("snatched away") to meet Jesus in the air (see 1 Thessalonians 4:15–17). The Latin word *rapturo* ("caught up") is where we get the term *rapture*.

The belief that Christ will rapture believers before the tribulation is consistent with the biblical pattern of God exempting believers from divine wrath:

- God delivered Lot out of Sodom (see Genesis 19:16).

- God delivered Noah from the flood (see 2 Peter 2:5).

- God delivered Rahab from destruction (see Joshua 6:17).

While believers are exempt from God's wrath during the tribulation (see 1 Thessalonians 1:10 and Revelation 3:10), we know that Christians should expect to go through trials, suffering, and persecution in life.

How should we live as we look forward to the Lord's return? Read Titus 2:11–14 and answer in your own words.

_____

_____

_____

_____

_____

_____

To "be ready" for Christ's return is to be faithfully obeying Him in the present, actively engaged in whatever work He has called us to.

—Wayne Grudem, Systematic Theology.[10]

  grow

Earthly Miseries and Heavenly Rewards

After the rapture, the world will plunge into an unprecedented time of turmoil and deep human misery. This is known as the great tribulation.

According to the prophecy of Daniel, this seven-year period will begin with a world leader who will appear to bring peace, but after 3½ years he will break his covenant with Israel (see Daniel 9:26–27). Showing his true colors, the Antichrist will control the world's inhabitants through the power of Satan (see 2 Thessalonians 2:9–11). But it will be the judgments of God poured out on wicked unbelievers that will make this the darkest time in history (Revelation 6–9, 16).

While the earth convulses under God's wrath, believers will stand before the judgment seat of Christ (see 2 Corinthians 5:10). An individual's salvation will not be in question here, since salvation is a free gift; but every person will be judged on the merit of their service to God and how they invested their earthly life (see 1 Corinthians 3:12–15). The Lord will test our works and reward each person accordingly. The Bible says that, "Each one's praise will come from God" (1 Corinthians 4:5).

The apostle Paul said he was running the race of life to receive an "imperishable" crown (1 Corinthians 9:25). What will be some of our heavenly rewards?

1 Thessalonians 2:19	The Crown of…	
James 1:12	The Crown of…	
2 Timothy 4:7–8	The Crown of…	
1 Peter 5:4	The Crown of…	

According to what we read in Revelation 4:9-11, what do you suppose we will do with our crowns?

> *Glory means good report with God, acceptance by God, response, acknowledgement, and welcome into the heart of things. The door on which we have been knocking all our lives will open at last.*
> —*C.S. Lewis, The Weight of Glory.*[11]

Christ's Earthly Return and Reign

"Now I saw heaven opened, and behold, a white horse. And He who sat on it was called Faithful and True, and in righteousness He judges and wages war." (Revelation 19:11)

At the end of the great tribulation, Jesus Christ will return to earth and there will be no mistaking who He is and what He comes to do. He will enter the scene of a fierce world war and conquer all the armies of earth (see Revelation 19:11–21; Zechariah 14:1–5). Satan will be chained in a bottomless pit and Jesus will begin His thousand-year reign on earth.

Some characteristics of life during this period will be:

- Resurrected believers will participate in this millennial reign (see Revelation 20:4).

- All humanity will enjoy peace, social justice, and personal safety (see Micah 4:3–4).

- The land will be a virtual paradise (see Joel 3:18).

- People will enjoy good health and long life (see Isaiah 32:3–4; Isaiah 65:20).

- Wild animals will be tame and harmless (see Isaiah 11:6).

When the millennial reign has been completed, the devil will be released and he will stir up rebellion in his final attempt at war with God.

The Final Judgment

Satan will make one last, futile challenge against God (see Revelation 20:8–9), but he and his followers will be swiftly destroyed by fire from heaven. Satan will be thrown into the lake of fire, where he will be "tormented day and night forever and ever" (Revelation 20:10). Resurrected non-believers will face judgment for their rejection of Jesus Christ, joining their deceiver in the lake of fire.

A Window into Eternity

Is heaven a state of mind? There are some who think so, but Scripture clearly teaches that heaven is an actual place, as real as the ground we tread through our fleeting years of earthly life. Jesus said, "I go to prepare a place for you, . . . And I will come again

 grow

and receive you to Myself, that where I am, there you may be also" (John 14:2–3). The last two chapters of Revelation are filled with beautiful descriptions of the new heaven and earth, yet it is only a small glimpse of eternity. Truth be told, even those descriptions are more than we can wrap our minds around.

"Let heaven fill your thoughts."
(Colossians 3:2 NLT)

Have you spent much time thinking about heaven? Many of us would have to admit that, apart from times of grief or suffering, the reality of heaven doesn't occupy our mind. Why should it? C.S. Lewis once said that the reason Christians have become so ineffective in this world is because they have ceased to think about the next one.

How will letting heaven fill our thoughts help us make a difference in the world today?

- It will give us the right perspective on life (see Philippians 3:20).

- It will inspire us to keep pressing on (see Philippians 3:13–14).

- It will cause us to walk wisely (see Ephesians 5:15–16).

- It will motivate us to keep ourselves pure (see 1 John 3:3).

- It will encourage us to keep our priorities straight (see Matthew 6:19–21).

- It will prompt us to share our faith (see 1 Peter 3:15).

ESTABLISHED IN THE FAITH

"As followers of Christ, we need to be living in such a way that we are ready for His return. . . . living in such a way that every moment counts. One day, each of us will be held accountable for how we spent our time, our resources, and our lives. Let's not waste them. Let's allow the anticipation of the Lord's imminent return to keep us on our toes spiritually."
—Greg Laurie, *For Every Season.*[12]

Last Days Events

Rapture of Jesus' Followers

1. Jesus will take believers to be with Him (see 1 Thessalonians 4:16–17).
2. No one knows the time or hour (see Matthew 24:44; Matthew 25:1–13).

Tribulation on Earth/Judgment Seat of Christ

1. The world will experience unprecedented turmoil (see Matthew 24:5–28).
2. Tribulation will continue for seven years (see Daniel 9:27).
3. Believers' works will be judged in heaven (see 1 Corinthians 3:10–15).
4. Horrors of tribulation will end with Christ's return (see Revelation 11–16).

Christ's Second Coming/Millennium Reign on Earth

1. Christ's victorious return will be witnessed by all (see Mark 13:24–26).
2. Satan will be bound; Jesus will reign for 1,000 years (see Revelation 20:1–6).

Judgment of Satan/Great White Throne Judgment

1. Satan will be judged and eternally punished (see Revelation 20:7–10).
2. Great White Throne judgment is for all nonbelievers (see Revelation 20:5).
3. Those not written in Book of Life will be judged (see Revelation 20:11–15).

New Heavens and New Earth

1. Heaven and Earth will pass away (see Matthew 24:35; Revelation 20:11).
2. God will create a new and dramatically different Heaven and Earth (see Revelation 21:1–22:5).

  grow

Notes

_____

_____

_____

_____

_____

_____

_____

_____

_____

_____

_____

_____

_____

_____

_____

_____

_____

_____

_____

_____

_____

_____

ABOUNDING

1. Would you say the knowledge that Christ could return at any time is something you think about frequently? Briefly share why, or why not.

2. What aspect of last days events do you find most difficult to understand? Has this chapter helped you gain a clearer picture?

3. Recite 1 Peter 4:7. What is one thing you will commit to lift up in prayer, for yourself and fellow believers, on a weekly basis?

Recommended Resources

Jensen, Irving L. *Revelation: A Self-Study Guide*, Revised Edition. Chicago, Ill. Moody Publishers, 1990.

Laurie, Greg. *Are These the Last Days?* Ventura, Calif.: Regal Books, 2005.

MacArthur, John. *The Second Coming*. Wheaton, Ill.: Crossway Books, 1999.

Walvoord, John. *The Rapture Question*. Grand Rapids, Mich. Zondervan Publishing, 1979.

grow

QUALIFICATIONS FOR SERVICE CHAPTER 8

ROOTED AND BUILT UP

So you want to serve the Lord. Good decision. Jesus said, "Come, follow Me . . . and I will make you fishers of men" (Mark 1:17 NIV)

The disciples didn't know it at the time, but Jesus' call was an invitation to participate in building His church. Little did they know that the remarkable life God chose for them would still be serving His purposes long after they finished their course.

It has been said that a man can count the seeds in an apple, but only God can count the apples in a single seed. What fruit will God bring forth out of your life of service?

In an orchard, the gardener's responsibility is to cultivate the ground and prune the trees to maximize their fruit-bearing capacity. Having done his part, he depends on God for the sun and rain to produce a successful harvest. So it is with serving the Lord.

As servants, our responsibility is to cultivate godly character. We yield to the seasonal need for pruning, disciplining ourselves for the purpose of godliness. Then we must depend on God to nourish our spirit and make us fruitful in service.

As Christians, we are all called to minister. Whatever your occupation in life may be, you are a minister. When we assume a role of service in the church, it is especially important that we pay close attention to our life and what we profess to believe. Salvation is a free gift that cannot be earned, but the Bible clearly teaches that those who serve must acquire credentials through obedience and holy living. The aim of this session is to lay out those qualifications as put forth in God's Word.

It isn't exceptional talent or ability that qualifies a believer to serve. It is a personal, growing knowledge of Jesus and willingness to call Him Lord, not just with our lips but with our life.

A Pure Heart, a Good Conscience, and a Sincere Faith

Character is like the foundation of a house, lying just below the surface of what is seen. But how we behave reveals what we value. When pleasing God is a high priority, our life and conduct will show it. The apostle Paul reminded Timothy what God looks for in a servant when he wrote, "But the goal of our instruction is love from a pure heart, a good conscience and a sincere faith" (1 Timothy 1:5 NASB).

What do you get when you have a pure heart, a good conscience, and a sincere faith? A holy life, which simply means a person God will use because he or she love and honor Him above all else. In terms of life and conduct, what are some of the qualities God looks for in a servant?

- **A blameless life.** The Bible instructs us to "be diligent to be found by Him in peace, without spot and blameless" (1 Peter 4:14). This describes an individual whose life and conduct is above reproach. The word *blameless* means "nothing to take hold upon." Though no person is sinless, we must not live in blatant, habitual sin.

- **Moral integrity.** "But immorality or any impurity or greed must not even be named among you, as is proper among saints" (Ephesians 5:3 NASB). This describes an individual who guards against sexual sin, lewd behavior, or an overindulgent desire for material possessions.

- **Trustworthy.** This describes an individual who is faithful, dependable, and can be relied on to keep their promises (see 1 Corinthians 4:2).

- **Humility.** Jesus Himself set the example for every servant when He said, "I am among you as the One who serves" (Luke 22:27). God looks for the individual who will serve others in a spirit of unity rather than seeking to promote their own agenda (see Philippians 2:3-4).

- **Love.** Jesus showed His disciples that love gets on its knees (see John 13:5). He made it clear that love would be the most powerful evidence the world could have that they were His servants (see John 13:34–35).

Cultivating godly character isn't a passive activity. In 1 Timothy 6:11, Paul commands Timothy to *pursue* ("hunt, chase after") character qualities that will please God and make an individual useful for service. List each quality and briefly explain how it can be put to practical use in service.

  grow

1. _____

2. _____

3. _____

4. _____

5. _____

6. _____

Discipline Yourself for the Purpose of Godliness

For a tree to continue bearing fruit year after year, it needs consistent maintenance and seasonal pruning. Left to itself, a tree becomes rangy. A wise gardener knows that branches must be gently forced into a more open canopy, so light can penetrate the center. As painful as it seems, pruning rejuvenates the life of the tree and spurs growth. Without regular, moderate pruning, a tree will stop bearing fruit. What a fitting illustration for the necessity of living a disciplined Christian life. Paul said, "Discipline yourself for the purpose of godliness" (1 Timothy 4:7 NASB).

> "Achieving anything requires discipline—determined, deliberate, definable actions with a clear goal in mind."
>
> —Charles Swindoll, So, You Want to be Like Christ?.[13]

Do you want to spread your branches wide and produce lasting fruit in your service for the Lord?

- **Be a student of God's Word.** "Be diligent to present yourself approved to God, a worker who does not need to be ashamed, rightly dividing the word of truth" (1 Timothy 2:15). The phrase *rightly dividing* means "cutting straight." God's Word cuts straight to the need of the heart (see Hebrews 4:12) whatever that need may be. Stray thoughts must be gently pinched back. Wrong concepts nipped in the bud. False notions lopped away. But a properly shaped tree requires more than pruning; healthy, pliable branches must be trained to grow in a direction that permits light to reach the center. One way to accomplish this is with spacers that consistently hold a young branch in position. In the same way, reading and obeying God's Word trains us to grow in the knowledge and grace of God.

- **Live a well-ordered life.** The apostle Paul was a man who aimed high and stayed focused. His life could be summed up in a phrase from Philippians 3:13, "One thing I do." We live cluttered lives. Too much fruit on a tree doesn't seem like a problem, but there's a downside. The tree's resources are stressed, which means you have to choose between a large harvest of puny fruit or a small harvest of robust fruit. Truth be told, the first casualty of a cluttered life is usually time spent with God. The wasting effect of a neglected inner life spreads outward, causing every branch to suffer. In laying out qualifications for church leaders, Paul describes a well-ordered life (see 1 Timothy 3:1–13; Titus 1:6–9, 2:2–8). These are desirable at tributes every believer should strive for.

Nourished on Sound Doctrine

Paul reminded Timothy that his responsibility as a servant and minister was to make sure that he himself was "constantly nourished on the words of the faith and of the sound doctrine" (1 Timothy 4:6 NASB). Sound doctrine simply means "complete, balanced teaching."

Unfortunately, some people have a tendency to "feed" on the Word as if it were a plate of appetizers. They pick and choose the parts they like best or find easiest to swallow. Such a haphazard approach isn't good for any Christian, but for those who assume a role of service in the church it is unacceptable. Whether your God-given ministry puts you in the pulpit or out in the parking lot, you need to make it your goal to read the entire Bible. This isn't a weekend project, but it is certainly attainable.

While there are different methods of studying the Bible, one essential rule governs them all. We cannot isolate parts of Scripture and take them out of context. That gets us into the same kind of trouble that Paul was addressing with Timothy in the following passage:

> "Preach the word of God. Be persistent, whether the time is favorable or not. Patiently correct, rebuke, and encourage your people with good teaching. For a time is coming when people will no longer listen to right teaching. They will follow their own desires and will look for teachers who will tell them whatever they want to hear. They will reject the truth and follow strange myths. But you should keep a clear mind in every situation." (2 Timothy 4:2–5 NLT)

In our opening thoughts, we stated that it is the servant's responsibility to cultivate godly character and discipline themselves for the purpose of godliness. But there is one qualification for service which is indispensable: we need the empowering of the Holy Spirit. Jesus Himself is our example.

> After being baptized, Jesus came up immediately from the water; and behold, the heavens were opened, and he saw the Spirit of God descending as a dove and lighting on Him, and behold, a voice out of the

 grow

heavens said, "This is My beloved Son, in whom I am well-pleased."
(Matthew 3:16–17 NASB)

Our Lord did not begin His earthly ministry without the anointing of the Holy Spirit. After His resurrection, Jesus instructed the disciples not to begin the work to which He called them until they were baptized in the Holy Spirit (see Luke 24:49; Acts 1:4, 8).

ESTABLISHED IN THE FAITH

"The same Spirit and the same anointing is available to us. We should not attempt what our divine Exemplar would not do—embark upon ministry without being anointed by the Spirit."

—J. Oswald Sanders, Shoe-Leather Commitment.[14]

Qualifications for Service

The Servant's Character

1. A servant must be above reproach (see 1 Timothy 3:2; 2 Peter 3:14).
2. A servant must have moral integrity (see Ephesians 5:3; 1 Thessalonians 4:7).
3. A servant must be trustworthy (see 1 Corinthians 4:2).
4. A servant must be humble (see Mark 10:42-45; Philippians 2:3–8).
5. A servant must demonstrate God's love (see John 13:34–35).

The Servant's Discipline

1. A servant must be a student of God's Word (see 2 Timothy 2:15, 3:16–17).
2. A servant must live a well-ordered life (see 1 Timothy 3:1–13; Titus 1:6–9, 2:2–8).
3. A servant must discipline themselves for godliness (see 1 Timothy 4:6–7).

The Servant's Guidelines

1. A servant must be Spirit-filled and Spirit-led (see Acts 6:3).
2. A servant must hold to sound doctrine (see 2 Timothy 3:14–15, 4:2–4).
3. A servant must be devoted to God's glory (see 1 Corinthians 3:4–7; Colossians 3:17; 1 Peter 4:2–4).

Notes

_____

_____

_____

_____

_____

_____

_____

_____

_____

_____

_____

_____

_____

_____

_____

_____

_____

_____

_____

_____

_____

_____

 ABOUNDING

1. Can you recall a time when you experienced spiritual pruning? Briefly share how it encouraged new growth and bore fruit in your life.

2. When you encounter a teaching that sounds good or seems to be popular, what steps do you take to verify that it is biblical?

3. What area(s) of ministry are you currently serving, or preparing to serve, in? What would you say you aim to accomplish there?

Recommended Resources

Sanders, J. Oswald. *Shoe-Leather Commitment.* Chicago, Ill.: Moody Publishers, 1992.

Sanders, J. Oswald. *Spiritual Leadership,* Revised Edition. Chicago, Ill.: Moody Publishers, 1994.

Swindoll, Charles. *So, You Want to be Like Christ?* Nashville, Tenn.: W Publishing, 2005.

Wiersbe, Warren. *On Being a Servant of God.* Grand Rapids, Mich.: Baker Book House, 1999.

NOTES

How to Study the Bible

1. Hendricks, Howard G. and William D. Hendricks. *Living By the Book* (Chicago, Ill.; Moody Publishing, 1991), p. 21.
2. Laurie, Greg. *For Every Season* (Dana Point, Calif.; Allen David Publishers, 2004), p. 151.

Salvation and Your Christian Witness

3. Tozer, A.W. *The Set of the Sail* (Camp Hill, Pa., Christian Publications, 1986) pp. 50–51.

Knowing God

4. Pink, A.W. *The Attributes of God* (Grand Rapids, Mich.; Baker Book House, 1991), p. 7.

The Work of the Holy Spirit

5. Torrey, R.A. *The Person and Work of the Holy Spirit* (Grand Rapids, Mich.; Zonder van Publishers, 1985), p. 102.
6. Wiersbe, Warren, ed. *The Best of A.W. Tozer* (Camp Hill, Pa.; Christian Publications, 1995), p. 208.

The Gifts of the Holy Spirit

7. Graham, Billy. *The Holy Spirit: Activating God's Power in Your Life* (Waco, Texas; W Publishing Group, 2000), p. 173.
8. Laurie, Greg. *The New Believer's Bible New Testament* (Wheaton, Ill.; Tyndale House, 1996), p. 241.

Spiritual Warfare

9. Tozer, A.W. *That Incredible Christian* (Camp Hill, Pa.; Christian Publications, 1986), p. 73.

Last Days Events

10. Grudem, Wayne. *Systematic Theology* (Grand Rapids, Mich.; Zondervan, 1994), p. 1,093.
11. Lewis, C.S. *The Weight of Glory* (New York, N.Y.; HarperCollins, 1949), p. 41.
12. Laurie. *For Every Season*, p. 235.

Qualifications for Service

13. Swindoll, Charles. *So, You Want to be Like Christ?* (Nashville, Tenn.; W Publishing Group, 2005), p. XI.
14. Sanders, J. Oswald. *Shoe-Leather Commitment* (Chicago, Ill.; Moody Publishers, 1992), p. 74.
15. Wiersbe, Warren. *On Being a Servant of God* (Nashville, Tenn.; Baker Books, 1999), p. 45.

 grow